Love Your Life
And
Expect The Best

Marlene Fuller Svoboda

Personal and Professional Life Coach
Ordained Interfaith Minister

ISBN: 9781655657023

Dedicated To

Mama
Gladys Viola Kingsbury Fuller
1914-2008

Who by her life taught me to
expect the best.

Acknowledgments

My husband, Tom, for being my encourager and publisher. My daughter, Samantha Kompier Guiher, for being my source of inspiration since the day she was born. My niece/editor, Sally Parker, for believing in me and lovingly taking on my first project. Rev. Joyce Rennolds, for being my teacher, mentor and friend. My supportive friends, Sheila Hughey, Barbara Nelson, Kathy Clester, Carol Antonino Rosenbusch and so many more who bring joy, peace, hope and gratitude to my very blessed life.

Contents

Introduction

Whatever your belief system, age, gender, or lifestyle, I hope you are a student of life and eager to expand your thinking. If there is one thought or lesson in this book you find helpful, gives you courage to make your best choices, or hope for your future, I am happy I wrote it and grateful it found its way into your hands.

Throughout this book, I will talk about God, divine intelligence, and divine wisdom. The purpose of this information is not to change your spiritual belief system, but to encourage you to connect with the creative higher power of your soul. I am sharing my experiences and insight, and my soul connection is God. It is up to each of us to take his or her own mental and spiritual inventory to uncover the lessons and purpose of our lives.

Life Experiences

Life experiences are very different, not only from one person to another in general, but from one person to another within a family. How we interpret our experiences and incorporate them in our lives helps form our identities, personalities and outlook on life. I am not a psychologist, but as a mature woman and the youngest of nine children, I have a lot of life experience. Our mother was the main breadwinner pretty much all my growing up years. She worked hard, and there was little time to sit down with her children and help shape their identities and personalities. Instead, our lessons came from witnessing Mama's work ethic, and her unrelenting sense of responsibility to do her best to feed, clothe and keep her children healthy. Each of us learned to be ethical in our work environments, and to be responsible for ourselves and our families. However, each of us interpreted many experiences very differently. We saw things through our individual lenses, which is what everyone does, family or not. As we matured, our interpretations may have changed, but we used them to create our own life experiences as adults.

As the youngest, I received a great deal of attention from my older siblings, but each one was anxious to grow up and strike out on their own. I felt abandoned. Of course, that was not their intent. I just felt that way. So, I wanted to strike out on my own as well. I didn't have a direction, though, or any real goals. As a result, my choices were not creating the life I wanted. I was working hard. I never broke the law, but I did find myself alone and the mother of a beautiful baby girl at the age of twenty. This was a turning point for me. I wanted more for my daughter than my thoughts, words and actions had created at that point. I began changing my outlook on life, and my life began to change. Still, I was young and had so much to learn. I began to see success in my future but didn't know exactly what that looked like. Each time I made a life choice that was not for my highest and best good, I promised myself I would look at the outcome, learn the lesson, and allow myself to move forward with courage. I learned from my past, but I did not let it define me. After two marriages and two divorces, I knew my mind, heart and soul were craving my attention. I had left a twenty-year career in the mortgage banking industry, gone back to school and emerged as a licensed massage therapist. These careers seem like polar opposites, right?! But they have more in common than it appears at first glance. In both fields I helped people achieve a goal. Whether it was to become a homeowner or learn to relax, enjoy a time of peace, or find pain relief, I found I loved helping others. As we pay attention to the effect our choices have, not only on our own lives but on the lives of others, we become more receptive to learning and growing.

Shortly after graduating from massage therapy school, I returned to the school bookstore. I had the knowledge and the skills to be a great therapist. My marketing skills had been well honed in my mortgage banking career, and I am a woman of faith, so I had prayed I would be able to develop my own practice. Still, I thought something was missing. So, there I stood, in the bookstore looking for that "something." I suppose, because I am an avid reader, I thought surely someone had written a book on "That Something You're Looking For." I did not find a book. What I was immediately drawn to instead was a set of cassette tapes by Rev. Dr. Joyce Rennolds, titled simply, "*Joyce Rennolds, Motivator of One or a Thousand*". Although I wasn't flush with money at the time, I bought the tapes because I have always believed I must be willing to invest in myself if I intend to grow. Purchasing those tapes turned out to be one of the best learning investments I have made. I couldn't wait to get in my car, pop in that first tape, and begin listening to what this woman I had never heard of had to teach me. When I opened the cover, there was a business card inside. Reading the card, I realized the author of the tapes was located about five miles from where I was sitting. I wanted to talk with her, and I hadn't even heard a word of her teaching! No, I didn't call Joyce at that moment. I did actually listen to a couple of her tapes first. When I called her later, I learned she offered weekly classes, and she invited me to come. This opened the door to an incredible learning and growing experience as well as a friendship of more than twenty years that continues today.

At first, I thought the principles I was learning may somehow be contrary to my faith or belief system. I was learning about energy, universal principles and the Law of Attraction. Were these supposed to replace God in my life, I wondered? The answer, in fact, was no! These are gifts made available to us by God, and God isn't "out there." God is in my soul and always has been. Whatever I think and speak about sends out energy to create more of it in my life. Worrisome thoughts create more problems in my life and leave me feeling drained. I believe that is true for most people. Knowing I am one with God allows me to think, speak and act in a positive way, creating a life of peace, joy and abundance. This is the Law of Attraction in a nutshell. What we send out into the world is what we attract back into our lives.

Because I believe I have the courage, strength, love, peace and joy of God within my soul, prayer is a way I live my life. We can call on God with hearts full of worry, or hearts full of faith. I don't believe God intends for me to beg, but to ask, walk in faith, and trust for the perfect outcome. The perfect outcome is what is for my highest and best good, and it happens in divine, right timing.

Throughout this book, I will talk about God, Divine Intelligence, and Divine Wisdom. If you believe your soul is connected to a different Higher Power, then call on the Higher Power as you are reading this material. The point is, there is a Universal Power, and it resides within the soul of each one of us and is the creative force in our lives. I am sharing my experiences and insight, and my soul connection is God.

In recent years we have heard a great deal about the body, mind and spirit connection. I was especially exposed to conversations about this connection in the world of massage therapy. While I understood the thought behind the discussions, I wondered why there was no mention of the soul. The soul is the creative, living part of us where God resides. It is where

God hears, knows and makes possible the lives we are intent on living. The soul lives on when all else passes away. The soul is God. This is exciting to me because I know when I want to create something new and wonderful in my life, I have all the resources I need: the courage, strength, wisdom, ability, patience and love of God to do it! Whether it is a new career, new or better relationships, healing, financial abundance or simply to pay this month's bills, I can claim that the Christ in me is making it manifest in my life now! How can I make such a bold statement? I could say it because I believed Divine Intelligence was working through me in each of the situations I mentioned and more. Because I thought it to be true, spoke it as my truth and scripted it in my journal, it demonstrated as truth in my life.

Let me tell you a little about scripting. (I devote a whole chapter to it later in the book.) As I mentioned, I had married and divorced twice. Scripting played a big part as I looked closely at both relationships and asked God to illuminate my role in them.

I scripted that I was open to learn the lessons I needed to learn, and to change the behaviors that needed changing so I could build healthier, stronger relationships in the future. Blame and guilt are life destroyers, not life builders. It is a healthy choice to acknowledge those behaviors we need to change and to understand it is only possible to change ourselves. I scripted that I would take all the time necessary to make healthy choices leading to positive, life-affirming change. I was single for several years. During this time, I built a successful massage therapy practice. With Joyce's encouragement, I completed a two-year ministerial program and became an ordained minister. I volunteered and offered a spiritual life program for women in an alcohol and drug addiction treatment program for five years. I became involved in a community merchants association, and my massage therapy practice continued to grow. Because I loved inspiring others to pursue their goals, I completed a Life Coaching course and I help my clients learn how to breathe life into their dreams using the principles I share in this book. I continue to apply these principles in my own life each day. I went out on dates, but the thought of another marriage was not one I entertained. All that I had been scripting for was being made manifest in my life.

During a time of prayer and meditation, it became clear to me just how important relationships are in my life and that someday I might want to share a loving, healthy, committed relationship with a man. So, I began by asking God to help me to want to be married again. I scripted this desire for a couple of years and found I knew the desire had grown in my heart. I then began scripting, in detail, the qualities that I would want in a husband. Trustworthiness was at the top of the list. It takes time to build trust in a relationship, so I began affirming that the man with those qualities important to me was coming into my life now, and that I would easily recognize him. Since I was in my forties at the time, I released all concern over the time it would take to build trust once I engaged with the man God was sending to me and drawing me toward. Here is the amazing, fun part of how the law of attraction, power of prayer, affirmation, and scripting all work together to create the lives we desire! I had an acquaintance who had become a friend over a three and a half year period. I had come to know him to be an honest, genuinely good person and had seen him handle some very difficult life situations with grace and in a prayerful manner. He and other friends had offered to help me move over a weekend. We all had fun as we worked hard to get my new home settled. By the end of the weekend, as he and I were sitting on my sofa sipping iced tea, he asked if he could kiss me. That was surely one of God's shining moments in both our lives. My answer, of course, was yes! We dated three years and then were married in a lovely ceremony officiated by Rev. Dr. Joyce Rennolds. That was over fourteen years ago, and we say prayers of gratitude each day for a blessed, loving life we co-created with divine guidance and through the law of attraction.

I share our story with you because I want you to know that no matter what your past looks like, you can choose to view it through a lens of success. You don't have to live your life looking through a rear view mirror. You can see yourself as courageous for having walked through it. You can use your courage, faith and powerful words of affirmation to create the life, relationships and opportunities you desire.

When we view our lives as a whole, allowing all experiences to teach us those aspects we want more of in life, we teach our thoughts, words and actions to focus on a positive outcome in each situation. If we parcel out and label our experiences as good or bad, we can go down a road of judgment, guilt, blame, approval or disapproval. When the mind wanders in this direction, we can affirm, "I release and let go of all negativity, now." Then, go for a better, more positive thought. The mind cannot hold two thoughts at one time, so be aware when you are feeling, thinking, speaking or acting negatively, and go for the positive feelings, thoughts, words and actions. It may take some practice, but it will change your life. When a negative thought creeps in, I may say something like, "No thanks. I release all negativity right now!" Just saying or thinking something like this puts a positive spin on a situation for me.

Our lives are filled with all kinds of experiences. Some we control, and some we don't. The key to drawing more of those experiences we desire is thinking, speaking and scripting about the positive lives we hope for and believing God is bringing them to us in divine timing. When we allow the mind's eye to see each life experience as a thread, weaving together with the others, our lives become a marvelous, beautiful quilt created by strength, joy, courage, gratitude and hope.

Our thoughts and words are powerful tools for creating our realities, and the written word is the most powerful. I have been scripting (some call it journaling) for many years and have volumes filled with my gratitude, goals and desires. I devote a whole chapter to scripting later in the book, but for now here's what you need to know: Scripting is to write as though you are already living the life you desire and believing that God is filling every area of your life with abundance now!

Relationships

My father-in-law left this earthly plane nine years ago, and I miss his insight, wisdom and humor. On more than one occasion, I heard him say that building good relationships was the foundation of a successful personal and professional life. He was right. How do we do that? What sort of relationships do you have, and are they the ones you want in your life? If not, read on, and let's explore the changes you can make that will attract and build healthy relationships.

We all have many relationship opportunities. What we think, feel and believe about ourselves is often reflected in the company we keep. As children, we were not responsible for what we were to think of ourselves. The adults in our lives—our families, teachers, religious leaders, neighbors— elevated or diminished us with their words and actions. Regardless of their intentions, we took their words and actions to heart. We believed them. I recall, on a second or third grade report card, my teacher wrote, "Marlene is a very good student, but she is a dreamer. The fact that I was a good student was lost, because the message I received was that being a dreamer was a negative. Imagine if the teacher had said, "Marlene is a very good student, *and* she is a dreamer." Wow! I would have believed differently about myself and my potential, and I will bet my mother would have, too. The point is, words are powerful. We cannot change what was spoken into our lives in the past, but we can think and speak words of affirmation about ourselves now. What we believe to be true about ourselves will be reflected in the relationships we attract and build. This is the law of attraction at work. Believe you are wise, strong, courageous, youthful, trustworthy, loving, loveable and successful, and you will attract others who possess these qualities and more.

If I share a personal or work environment with a negative person, I love, bless and release them to their highest and best good. Of course, I do not walk up to them and say, "I love bless and release you to your highest and best good." Here's how it works: I send the thought to them, and I often write it in my journal. I may have to say, think and write it several times before I truly feel the burden of their negativity has been lifted. Sometimes, the law of repulsion kicks in, which takes one of us out of the situation altogether.

Because I believe I am one with God and God is one with me, I know I have the strength and compassion to release my judgment of another's negativity and to reject their judgment of me. Strong, healthy relationships cannot grow in a critical, judgmental environment. Everything we think and do requires energy. Pouring positive energy into a negative situation is life draining, not life building. We can change the way we think and act, but we cannot change the thoughts and actions of others.

Building a relationship requires the positive investment of two people. It is a two-way street. It also requires authenticity. When we can trust and are trustworthy, it opens a door for each person to share and invest more in the relationship. Each of us may experience many relationships in a lifetime. Some will go deeper and last longer than others. Whether it is a friendship, a loving partnership or a professional relationship, it is up to us to offer qualities of trust, respect and honor and to know we deserve these same qualities in return.

Long-term relationships have periods of growth and plateaus. Sometimes, one person may be investing more in the relationship than the other. We will have opportunities to comfort, support and perhaps care for one another in healthy ways. We can also ask for and receive the wisdom to know when we should allow the people in our lives the time and space to care for themselves. Having healthy boundaries allows a relationship to exist and grow. Crossing these boundaries may invite enabling behavior, so be sure to affirm clarity and discernment of your choices and actions in relationships.

Are you a good communicator? I ask, because communication is so important in building both personal and professional relationships. Simply put, communication means you talk, and I listen. I talk and you listen. If we are thinking ahead about what we want to say, we are going to miss much of what the other person is saying. What we miss may be very important building blocks for our relationship. More success comes our way in business when we have listened to what our client, patient or customer needs and wants from us. Deeper, richer, more intimate personal relationships develop and grow when we have listened with intent to the desires, concerns and opinions of friends, children, parents, partners, wives and husbands. If I find I am wanting to interrupt someone else, I affirm my desire to be courteous and focused. There are also times I affirm courtesy and focus for others in a conversation. The quality of every aspect of our lives, including relationships, depends on what we are feeding our minds, and believing we may expect the best.

Choices

Our choices are the building blocks of our lives. The base or foundation we build on is our belief system. Because I believe God is my strength, courage, hope and joy, I feel a firm foundation as I build my life one block, or one choice, at a time. Several years ago, I was teaching a class and discussing this very subject, when one of my students raised his hand and said, "I don't have a belief system. I think I am doing life on my own." My response to him was that he does, in fact, have a belief system, and it says there is no Higher Power that provides energy, strength or hope. No Higher Power to help create our dreams and allow us to trust the process, and then deliver them with perfect timing. No Higher Power to trust for healing and abundance in every area of our lives. I believe God makes a home in the very core of my being--my soul. For me, that is a foundation that cannot be cracked or shattered by the strongest of earthquakes. So, as we make choices and build the structure of our lives, we need to know the strength of our foundation.

Our choices may change over time. We may replace one building block with another, and we need to know our foundation will support us through these changes. So before we delve into some of the many opportunities for choice in life, please take as much quiet, meditative, prayerful time as you need to understand what your belief system is, how or if it supports you, and if you are willing to invite it into the co-creation of your best life.

The actual process of making choices is quite simple. Our choices are made using the conscious mind. The information used to make choices is stored in the subconscious mind. How did the information get in the subconscious? We put it there with our thoughts, beliefs and focus. It is a bit like a GPS. We store all kinds of information/data in the subconscious mind, and when we need direction in making a choice, the conscious mind retrieves what we have stored in the subconscious mind. For example, let's say you have a goal to receive a promotion at work, and you have stored beliefs that you are not qualified, not smart enough, not old enough or not young enough. That is the information you will retrieve, and you will probably make the choice to not pursue your dream even if an opportunity arises. On the other hand, if you believe you have the experience and knowledge needed, that your age is no barrier to good performance, and that you have the courage to put your hat in the ring, your promotion will come to you in divine timing.

If you have been caught in a web of negative thinking, you have the power to flip that switch off! I know this is true, because I have done it myself. When negative thoughts are urging you not to make your best life choices, look them in the eye and release them. An affirmation like "I live the life I love, and I have the courage, ability and wisdom to make healthy choices that support me" will replace negativity in your subconscious mind, and your conscious mind will recall it again and again. Own your positive, life-affirming thoughts, and speak them out loud. Like a muscle, this practice grows stronger with use. (For more affirmation ideas, see a list of my favorites at the end of the book.)

A few years ago, I experienced a sudden, prolonged period of ill health. Every day, I spoke, prayed and scripted these words: "God is healing me perfectly and completely, now! I am learning patience with myself and compassion for others." I also affirmed that I took the action required on my part to be restored to health.

Remember, I believe I am co-creating this great life with God, so yes, there is action required on my part. During the illness I mentioned, there were many prescriptions necessary in the healing process. Some side effects were unpleasant, and I had to reach deep into my subconscious mind where I found a huge reserve of stored gratitude. I brought that gratitude into my conscious mind where I created the following thoughts then spoke and wrote these words: "I am grateful for the wisdom of my physician and for this medicine. I take it as prescribed knowing my healing is taking place. Thank You, God." The medical journals did not believe that healing was possible, but God and I had chosen a different, more positive outcome. My physician came to believe my healing was taking place as well, and our conversations were open, honest and always positive.

Allow your mind to focus and create positive, life-building, grateful thoughts. They will be stored in your subconscious mind for your conscious mind to recall whenever you have a choice to make.

Courage

By definition, courage is the ability to do that which frightens us. Merriam-Webster Dictionary defines courage this way: "mental or moral strength to venture, persevere, and withstand danger, fear, or difficulty." Apparently, this word has been in use since the fourteenth century. I find it interesting that for about seven hundred years we have understood the meaning, strength and power of the word "courage" and have called on it in a multitude of life situations. Where does courage come from when we have suffered the loss of a loved one or relationship? Where do we find courage to ask for or allow forgiveness, or to step out of our comfort zones and use talents we know we possess but have been too afraid to try? When we face debilitating illness, where do we find courage to dispel fear and anxiety? And where do we find courage to say no to judgment (ours or others), guilt, fear or pretense, and say yes to living a life of authenticity?

I have lived long enough to have faced many situations requiring courage. I needed a strength to persevere or make a choice that only courage could accomplish. Yes, like most people, my initial loss, fear or doubt seemed insurmountable in the face of these challenges, but I learned a long time ago that those rascals are greedy. The more thought we give them, the more of our thoughts, time and energy they demand. We spiral further and further down into a pit of loss, fear, doubt and anxiety. When we know our power to change our thinking is in the moment, we can claim the courage, strength and divine wisdom of God. We can open our hearts and our minds to claim and accept healing, faith and confidence.

A few years ago, when I was very ill, I had to claim my courage every day, often several times a day. I did not do it with a lengthy prayer either. I kept it simple, but powerful. I affirmed: "God is healing me *now*, and I am grateful." I even wrote it on sticky notes that I posted in each room where I could see them. Our statements of courage do not need to be lengthy or complicated. They need to be powerful, and we need to be open to accept the results that will come to us in small and big ways through Divine Intelligence. Walking in faith is the manifestation of courage. We step out in faith in the knowledge that there is a divine safety net, not only beneath but all around us. We are not tied to the results, but we believe in the divine right outcome, at the divine right time. Courage is believing the strength of God is doing with us what we cannot do alone. We do not have to wage a war against illness, loss, fear or doubt; we just claim the strength and courage of God to take the next right action as the divine outcome appears.

We all know people who complain endlessly about how difficult life is, how unlucky they are, how unfortunate their childhood was, how they always attract losers in their relationships or believe they are destined to experience poor health. The list goes on and on, but you get the idea. You have heard the person who says, "If it weren't for bad luck, I would have no luck at all." They may even laugh as they say this, but the truth is, it is no laughing matter. We know how powerful our thoughts and words are, and they are creating more of exactly what they claim not to want. Whining and complaining is toxic, not only to those doing it, but also to those allowing themselves to listen to it. Another person's negative talk can leave you feeling drained of your positive energy. This is an opportunity for you to step out in courage and excuse or remove yourself from the presence of a negative person. You may hear someone say they have "turned a problem over to God," and yet they continue worrying or speaking negatively about the issue. Maybe this is you. If it is, try this affirmation: "I release this issue to Divine Intelligence and am open to receive a divine outcome in divine right timing." The rewards of stepping out and speaking out in courage are peace, joy and a life of enduring abundance. Life will still present challenges, but knowing we have the courage and strength of the divine to navigate them gives us hope as we keep our eyes on the horizon for the divine right outcome.

Spirituality

Spirituality covers a broad spectrum today. It may be used to define deep, religious values and traditions for one person, while to another it may mean a deep, soulful connection to a higher power, guiding light, God or Divine Intelligence. To still another, it may be a combination of all of these or something completely different. I even know people who say they do not believe, but that they want to believe, because there is no other explanation for certain life events or experiences. My personal opinion is that if a person wants to believe in a spiritual dimension or influence, they already do. They simply have not learned how to allow Spirit to work with them in creating the lives they desire.

Learning to connect with spiritual power that is, I believe, available to each of us takes practice and study. That is true of most ideas we value and want to incorporate into our lives. There are spiritual practices we may include daily that will open the soul and reveal our higher power, God, guiding light and Divine Intelligence. We must first expand our thinking and understand the God of our soul is an unlimited source of power and energy in every area of our lives.

Each of us must find spiritual truth for ourselves. Spiritual leaders may teach and inspire us, but we must do the work and be open to the wisdom. Just as each person has similar as well as different physical and emotional needs and desires, they have similar and different spiritual needs and desires. I will attempt to map the journey of spiritual growth from the initial spark and desire to discover one's own spiritual base, through developing belief and value systems to the point where they are incorporated into daily life and lived out with ease, love and grace.

The spark that ignites spiritual desire may come out of disaster or from a profoundly wonderful life experience. On the other hand, it may be as simple as curiosity. Whatever the source, it is important to know that everyone has a rich spirit just waiting to be awakened.

People often fail to realize that infinite wisdom and divine power are always available. Instead, they wait for sickness or calamity to access this power. In his book *The Sermon on the Mount*, Emmet Fox wrote, "As a rule, it is only when health is broken down, and ordinary medical means have failed to afford relief, that people seriously set about gaining that spiritual understanding of the body as the true embodiment of Divine Life that is our only guarantee of overcoming sickness and, ultimately, death. Yet, if people would turn to God and acquire something of this understanding while their health is still good, they need never be sick at all." (p 24 par 1) Certainly, there are times the spiritual spark begins when something wonderful occurs, such as the birth of a child. This may bring a new or renewed interest in making positive life choices, and one of these choices may be to seek a higher power for guidance. Very often I encounter people who simply feel there is a void in their lives, and their spark is one of curiosity. They begin a quest to find out what is available for them on a spiritual level.

Whatever the spiritual spark may be there is a commonality for each person. They are all seeking wisdom. They may not understand this in the beginning of their journey. In fact, they may claim to be seeking knowledge. This is because, at this point in their spiritual growth, it is hard for them to see the difference between knowledge and wisdom. Knowledge is information we gain through study or training. It is valuable and applicable in specific areas of life. Many people who are not particularly interested in spiritual pursuits are very knowledgeable individuals. On the other hand, wisdom is universal, born of a higher power. It pours lovingly, gracefully and honestly from the spirit, not simply from the mind. The book of Proverbs in the Bible (chapter eight, verse eleven) says, "Wisdom is more precious than rubies, and nothing you desire can compare with her." Knowledge often seeks to prove or disprove something, and in so doing can create turmoil and unrest. This is why thinking your way through a problem often doesn't lead to a solution. Wisdom brings peace, love and serenity, which open new possibilities. In *As a Man Thinketh*, James Allen wrote, "Calmness of mind is one of the beautiful jewels of wisdom." (p 50 par 1) If we truly open to hearing our wisdom, we open to the serenity of the spirit, and our spiritual journey has begun.

As we move along the spiritual path, we soon discover the impact of our thoughts and choices on the developments or demonstrations in our lives. At this point we start to identify our belief and value systems and make choices that will support them behaviorally. In other words, if a person says that he/she believes a healthy body, mind and spirit are important, and that it is his/her responsibility to nourish and honor them, is he/she making choices that support this behaviorally? Perhaps you say you value your family, but you spend twelve hours each day at work and have no energy remaining for them when you get home. You may even have convinced yourself that you are working all the time for your family. I have no doubt you love your family, but your behavior says you value work more. Dividing up the pie of life can be confusing. That is why it is essential to get very clear about our values. The best method for doing this is through prayer and meditation. If we go to our divine source of wisdom and power and ask for clarity, it will come with ease. Clarity reveals that our spirituality must be the basis for every choice we make in life. Our spirit contains our wisdom. Unlike the mind, which may know a thing and then forget it, the spirit never forgets. Therefore, we can call on it at any time for guidance and we will receive it. There is no need to demand or plead for what we want. God wants us to receive what is good and perfect for our lives. All that is required of us is to ask, and then be patient. There are certain universal spiritual laws in effect, one of which is the law of least effort. In *The Seven Spiritual Laws of Success*, Deepak Chopra calls this law "the principle of least action, of no resistance." (p 53 par 1) We often try so hard to make things happen. We try to force an outcome, never consulting Divine Intelligence. The result is frustration, or feelings of failure and guilt. When we seek spiritual guidance, we realize how effectively the law of least effort really works.

In *Stake Your Claim*, Emmet Fox wrote, "Realization is the key to demonstration." ("Stake Your Claim" p 43 par 2) We must all come into Truth on our own. While spiritual teachers certainly serve to help and guide us on our journey, ultimately the answers lie within our own souls. It is up to each of us to take our own mental and spiritual inventory to uncover the lessons and purpose of our lives. We should understand that our realization of Truth will not come to us until we are completely open to receive it. This is a critical key in every aspect of life, because our outward demonstrations come through realization. Realization is that "aha" moment when we suddenly have clarity and understanding of something that had previously eluded us. We often hear a person claim they had an epiphany about a certain thing or situation. This may be a spiritual realization. They see clearly how different thoughts and choices will create a more desirable outcome. They are experiencing spiritual growth and soon begin to realize how important their own thoughts and words are in deliberately creating the lives they desire and the person they desire to be.

There are volumes written on the power of our thoughts and words in the creation of our lives, and yet I believe enough cannot be said on the subject. Limiting thoughts will limit our growth in life. Negative, unhealthy thinking attracts unpleasant people and situations as well as sickness and injury. As Catherine Ponder points out in her book *The Dynamic Laws of Prosperity*, Hippocrates, the fourth-century Greek physician, wrote: "Men ought to know that from the brain, and from the brain only, arise our pleasure, laughers and jests, as well as our sorrows, pains, griefs and fears." Ponder also pointed to Plato, who declared, "If the head and body are to be well, you must begin by curing the soul." (p 393 par 2) The Bible also speaks to the power of thought on life and health, when in Proverbs (chapter 17, verse 22), Solomon writes, "A cheerful heart causes good healing. But a broken spirit dries up the bones." It is important to realize that we are the masters of our minds, and the mind does not think a single thought unless we allow it. How often we hear someone say, "I always get colds and the flu, etc.", and sure enough, they often have a cold, flu or some other physical affliction. Inspirational author James Allen wrote, "The body is the servant of the mind. Whether they be deliberately chosen or automatically expressed, disease and health, like circumstances, are rooted in thought."

If our thoughts are important to our physical and spiritual growth, then we must know that our written and spoken word is very powerful. The first point I would make here is that we should speak and write about what we do want, not what we do *not* want. We create more of whatever it is we talk about, so to say, for example, "I do not want to get sick" may actually attract illness. The reason this is true is that we are creating from a place of fear and negativity rather than peace and positive energy. Instead of "I do not want to get sick" we might say, "I am healthy and strong." This takes practice for most of us as we are growing spiritually and allowing infinite wisdom to guide us. Affirmative journaling is an excellent method of training our positive thought and word nature to emerge. We begin to see and experience outward manifestations and demonstration very quickly. Some of these demonstrations may be small, but because we are becoming increasingly aware of the power of Spirit within to create outwardly, we no longer miss our miracles—large or small. We start seeing them everywhere. Just as Emmet Fox wrote in *Stake Your Claim*, "Negative thinking only begets more negative thinking, and we simply keep on producing more and more negative conditions,"

(Stake Your Claim" p 29 par 2), the same is true of our words.

It is not hard work to grow our spiritual lives, and we do not want to make it so, but it does require practice as is true with any gift or talent. The best way to practice is through the development of our daily prayer and meditation time or times. This is very personal and will be different for each of us. It may simply be a time of silence for some—a time to clear the mind, to listen to the spirit, to just "be." It could be a time of positive visualization for others. During this time, the person actually "sees" and affirms his own spiritual growth being outwardly demonstrated. It may be a time of prayer for the individual to ask God for peace, serenity and spiritual understanding. It could also be a time of contemplative prayer. The Cistercian monks practiced this type of prayer as they went to a place of "no thought." They did not talk to God. They gently cleared their minds of all thought, and simply listened for God's Wisdom to speak to them. When thoughts inevitably come up, we briefly notice and then let them go without following them. As we can see, how we practice our spiritual growth is a personal choice, and one that is essential as we continue our journey and seek our spiritual truth. Emmet Fox called this practice our "setting-up exercises" and said, "Whatever you do, you should never neglect your regular spiritual setting-up exercises." ("Stake Your Claim" p 52 par 5)

This is what happens when we regenerate the soul: Everything in our lives shifts. Our global perspective changes, because we are viewing the world from a more positive perspective. Our health and even our physical appearance improve because the body mirrors the soul. As we begin to radiate peace, serenity and unconditional love, we find we attract more of it through the situations and people in our lives. Really wanting peace and feeling it in the heart is how this regeneration begins. We cannot attract anything outwardly that we do not already possess inwardly.

People often seek self-improvement outside themselves, as though they are defective in some way. They look for someone who will disclose the secret that will make them better, smarter, richer or more attractive, when all the while they possess in their very own soul all the necessary ingredients for their spiritual journey, leading them to all the health, happiness, success and prosperity they desire and deserve.

As we grow spiritually stronger, we realize how important it is not only to think, write and speak the desires of our hearts but also to believe we deserve to receive them. This is a difficult concept for some people. Often, we think because we give freely of our time, talents and gifts we are living a spiritual life. I wish to be very clear: Giving certainly is an important part of spiritual growth, but the other half of giving is receiving. If we do not allow others to give to us, if we are not open to receiving, the effect is two-fold: We deny someone else the gift of giving, and we stunt our own spiritual growth because we are saying, in essence, "I am not deserving." This is not a spiritual truth.

One way to open our hearts and minds to receive is to ask God to help us to live our lives from a point of love, peace and grace. When we do this, we are not only able to give freely and with a loving spirit, but we are willing to be gracious, grateful receivers as well. Giving and receiving helps nurture and strengthen our spirits and brings a peace to our souls.

This peace enhances the overall serenity of life that encourages the development of what Emmet Fox called poise. "Poise," he wrote, "is a mark of the spiritual life. In addition, it is the key to happiness." ("Stake Your Claim" p 57 par 1) Poise is the mark of a life lived with ease and grace. It requires slowing down, living in the present moment and being focused and balanced. Poise is not attained through hard work or scattered thinking. It comes through practicing the law of least effort. Your spiritual poise is recognized by others as you radiate a quietness and calmness. When we possess spiritual poise, anger and fear rarely besiege us. Even in emergency situations, the poised individual remains calm, focused and totally present in the moment. Poise is a spiritual knowing that infinite power and wisdom are our guides. As we grow spiritually, we will find our poise to be very natural and comfortable, bringing with it greater peace and joy than we have ever experienced.

Spiritual discovery and growth occur in different ways and at a different pace for each of us. When we open our hearts, minds and souls to this growth, we must allow it to permeate every aspect of life. Every choice, every relationship and every situation must be seen as a spiritual growth opportunity. We are to look for the lessons we are to learn from each of these and ask God to help us learn and grow. Spiritual growth is ongoing. The spirit is always evolving, and we must remain open to all the possibilities. Our health, peace, love and happiness depend on our developing the spiritual habit of seeking infinite wisdom and claiming it as our own. When we do this, we free ourselves from the conditional love and judgments of anyone, including ourselves. Additionally, we are able to offer nonjudgmental, unconditional love to others. We do not barricade ourselves from the world, but neither do we attach emotionally to the issues and challenges of others. This allows us to hold them up in prayer and thought even more effectively and to release them to infinite wisdom for healing and guidance.

As we find ourselves maturing spiritually, we realize there is always more to learn. If there were not, we would not be here. When we fill our hearts with divine love, we welcome the learning process with great anticipation. Fear, anger guilt and doubt leave us, and healing takes place in our bodies, our relationships and our business affairs.

No matter what your concept of God or Higher Power is, you come to realize that it is a power you have within, not some elusive force outside yourself. We cultivate this strength and patience to face and succeed in all life offers us.

Our spiritual journey is a personal one, but it need never be a lonely one. As we live our lives with peace, love and grace, we will naturally attract more of the same. Our relationships will reflect this. Our life purpose will become very clear, and we will enjoy success, prosperity and happiness in every area, even through life's inevitable changes.

We should not covet another's spiritual growth. This demeans our own and implies we are somehow not good enough. "This Spiritual Coming of Age cannot be hurried or forced, but must appear in its own good time, when the consciousness is ready," Emmet Fox wrote in *The Sermon on the Mount*. "You have to demonstrate where you are." (p 53 par 1) Others may have spiritual knowledge to share with us, but we must be focused only on what God and infinite wisdom are teaching us right here, right now. There is a saying: "When the student is ready, the teacher will come." Your teachers and mine already exist and are simply waiting for us to be ready to learn. There will be times our spiritual growth may seem to be happening quickly, and others when it is noticeably slower. Some of our life lessons will take longer to learn than others. Our responsibility is to remain open and willing to learn them. Our spiritual growth is our whole reason for being. Florence Scovill Shinn said, "True Spirituality is proving God as your supply daily—not just once in a while." When we seek divine wisdom and are receptive to God's power within us, it is a wonderful journey.

Peace

Peace. Just the thought or sound of this word has a calming effect on my mind which then brings balance to my whole being. Peace creates fertile ground for our souls to flourish, our thoughts to expand and our hearts to feel the presence of God or Divine Intelligence. My sister has said she often begins a time of prayer by simply saying the word "peace" as a way of inviting God into her intimate prayer space.

But peace is much more than a quieting of the mind and body. It is an agent of change and renewal. In fact, it is also the inspiration for a life lived on purpose. Pay attention to people who enjoy a successful career, have a healthy, happy personal life, and are spiritually connected to their divine source of power. They are not driven by some erratic source of power, stealing time from one important area of life to feed another. Instead, their lives flow, as they are guided by Divine Intelligence. They easily and with intention set priorities and live their lives on purpose. Is life occasionally interrupted for them? Absolutely. But they do not run around like a whirling dervish trying to stomp out fires. They recognize their need to get recentered, invite Divine Intelligence into the process and to seek guidance and resolution.

Let's face it: Life happens all over us sometimes. We face illness, lose a loved one, receive a low grade on a test or lose a job opportunity. We do not want these situations to throw our lives into permanent chaos, so it is vitally important that we take time every day to nurture our peaceful nature. Doing this strengthens our ability to find peace in life's difficult circumstances.

So, how do we create a space for peace to live and thrive? It's simple. Perhaps we do as my sister does and simply sit quietly and say the word "peace," allowing ourselves to feel the presence of the divine. Or, we could focus on our breathing and feel our heartbeat slowing and our mind and body coming back to a place of homeostasis/balance. As you heighten your desire for peace, you will discover the opportunities and situations that give you a sense of peace. You will not be willing to forfeit or compromise them because you realize peace is an integral part of a purposeful life.

Being aware of our personal conditions for peace is important. We are not one size fits all when it comes to experiencing peace. For example, in our living room my husband and I have a number of pillows on the sofa. Some support our backs, and we place others on the coffee table where we prop our feet as we watch TV. The TV is behind folding doors when not in use. My husband is a very neat man, but at the end of an evening of TV watching, he wants to go straight to bed and sometimes groans a bit when I start putting pillows, tables and doors back in place. I also make sure the TV is set back to the soothing music channel. I have shared with him that a big part of creating my peace first thing in the morning is orderliness and turning on the soothing music channel. I begin my day with prayers of gratitude when I wake up. I ease out of bed and immediately make the bed because, for me, again, orderliness creates peace. I am certainly not the neat police, but I have been in homes where things were so disheveled the inhabitants could not find a thing. It was chaotic, and there was no room for peace. I will tell on myself. I do not do my writing at the desk in my office. My desk is not the most orderly spot in our home, and it is where I do my linear thinking and take care of business. It does not provide the peace I require for creative writing that I find at the kitchen table. From this table I enjoy the peace of our cozy, mostly organized kitchen, and I have lots of windows looking out on our yard, woods and a pasture where deer stop by to graze or nap. I also have windows to our sunroom where our two cats, Libby and Olivia, eat, nap and repeat. No one knows how to find peace quite like a cat, I am sure. Our kitchen table is a very peaceful, creative spot.

I encourage you to catch yourself feeling peaceful. Pay attention and make a note of where you are, what you are doing and how wonderful you feel. Then, find ways to recreate those situations or acts that welcome peace into your life.

Love

I am by no means an authority on love. I do believe each of us has a tremendous capacity for love, though. Whether we allow love to manifest and demonstrate in our lives is up to us. There are any number of reasons why we may not allow ourselves to love or be loved, but I would rather focus on some of the reasons we should love and accept love from others. Some people may have had their trust betrayed and believe they cannot love without trust, but I have come to realize that love and trust are two separate expressions. Because I send love to someone does not necessarily mean I take them into my circle of trust. Whom we love and how we love them is up to each of us to determine. Loving and accepting love is, I believe, important in the nurturing of our mental, emotional, physical and spiritual health. Love is also instrumental in our personal and professional success. Catherine Ponder taught something I have proven to be true in my own life: Love is born not only from our thoughts and feelings, but from our expectations as well. As a matter of fact, it is exactly that wisdom that produced my title for this book and my desire to share the thoughts and principles I use to create my own fabulously blessed life.

So, a good place for me to begin this discussion about love and its important impact on our lives is to invite you to put yourself on your schedule. Set aside some time, at least an hour but more if you can, to mentally review your life. If you are at all like me, an hour will not be nearly enough to look into all the nooks and crannies at all the bits and pieces of life you have lived. I found writing my life story to be helpful, but whatever is most effective for you is what you should do. Just do not leave anything out of your story. Before beginning your journey down memory lane, sit quietly for a few minutes in loving appreciation of yourself for setting out on this journey. Give yourself permission to love your life experiences and the lessons you have learned without judging anything or anyone as good or bad, right or wrong. Taking this introspective journey was an illuminating experience for me. It helped me understand how each experience, choice and person has brought me to this moment in my life, to be doing what I am doing. I learned that by loving my life—all of it—and expecting the best, I create a loving energy that not only helps me live and enjoy my best life personally and professionally but generates loving energy toward others.

Loving energy is powerful. When we love ourselves, we produce more love to generate. We can ask God's divine love to be directed to all sorts of circumstances, relationships, personal and professional opportunities and even where healing is needed. Our love may be personal and directed to someone through our expression of devotion, trust and appreciation. On a universal level, we may send love to everyone and be open to receive it from everyone. This sets us up to transition smoothly throughout our daily experiences and interactions with others.

Invoking divine love can calm heated tempers and bring resolution. Sending divine love where there is illness or injury may restore health. Asking divine love to bring forgiveness can restore a relationship. Saying or writing affirmations of love each day, throughout the day, creates peace and fosters the growth of more love. An affirmation such as "I send love and blessings to everyone I encounter today" opens the door for the law of attraction to bring wonderful people to your path, resolutions to problems and abundance to your life and the lives of others.

We do not know where others are or what they may be facing in their journey, and we do not need to know the details. We can still send divine love to them that can ease their pain, help them cope with grief or find financial freedom. God's divine love is endless. Be open to receive it and willing to share it with others without exception.

Expressions of love are important, so tell your family, spouse, children and close, personal friends that you love them. It blesses them to hear it, and it blesses us to say it. Of course, it is not appropriate to say "I love you" to business associates or to the salesperson who just helped you find that perfect gift for your significant other, but we can express impersonal love through courtesy and words of appreciation. People often take the time to write a letter or place a phone call to report their dissatisfaction with a rude or inefficient employee, but how about writing a letter of appreciation for the courteous, patient, knowledgeable employee who helped resolve a problem or successfully answered your question? Write that letter of appreciation. It is an act of love that may bolster their self-esteem or may be just what was needed to secure a promotion.

Love is not something to be earned but should be freely given. Unfortunately, some children are taught or made to believe they must earn love and that it can be revoked when their behavior is not suitable to the person acting as the love police. I loved my daughter from the moment I knew she was being formed, and the first time I held her I felt more love than I ever imagined could exist. When my daughter was three years old I married a man who, we soon learned, believed we had to earn his love. To be very clear, this is not love at all but is clearly cruel manipulation. Fortunately, God's love for and through me taught me how to love myself and my daughter with a strength and courage that took us out of that relationship and into our truly blessed lives. As my daughter grew up, I assured her I always loved her, even when I did not like her behavior. I think that is important for us to know as adults as well. When we behave badly, we need to acknowledge it, seek forgiveness, forgive ourselves and know the love of those closest to us has not been withdrawn. The wonderful truth of love is that the more we allow ourselves to send and receive love, we find less and less of the bad behavior manifested in ourselves and others. People do not always agree, but when we lovingly consider our options, there is always a resolution available. When my husband, Tom, and I disagree, I ask myself this question: "Do I want to be right more than I love Tom?" The answer is always no.

Divine love holds the answers to every situation we face in this life. When we send healing love to another and they leave this life, that is their healing. Divine love is also, then, available to heal the grief we feel for the physical loss of our loved one. In every life situation, affirm, "Perfect results of divine love now appear."

Gratitude

The title I chose for this book is the short version of my definition of gratitude: "Love Your Life and Expect the Best." You may be wondering how a person can love their entire life when some pretty unlovely things have happened on the road to where you are. It would make sense to love most, or much, or part of life, but all of it? Yes, all of it! When we can look at the life we have lived without praise or blame, but with gratitude for the wonderful experiences as well as gratitude for the lessons learned from the difficult times, we create the space, mindset and ability to expect the best now and in the future.

Some people may seem more naturally grateful, or you may believe others have more reason to be grateful. The truth is, no one travels through life without experiencing heartache, loss, betrayal or other negative or hurtful situations. It is how we choose to walk through those experiences that makes the difference. Gratitude improves our mental outlook. It can help us deal with our emotions more positively, and it can help us grow spiritually. Being grateful for the courage to walk through difficulty or pain helps our healing process. If you have not developed an attitude of gratitude, it takes practice, as do most worthwhile personality traits. It is easier to be grateful for the "good" things, so start there. Just notice. For example, the perfect parking space opens up, someone holds a door for you, you receive a raise or a compliment. This will give you plenty of opportunities every day to express gratitude. I must warn you that you will also become keenly aware of your behavior or mindset when the unlovely situations arise. That's a good thing! It is an opportunity for you to mentally release any negative feelings and to express gratitude for the courage to walk through a challenge and learn the lesson it has to teach you. What we learn may be a blessing to our lives and, best of all, may allow us to be a blessing in the future to someone else.

Grateful people tend to be happier. According to a number of studies, they are healthier, too. They are vibrating or resonating at a higher energy level than those who are ungrateful. A high energy level encourages us to take care of ourselves. Grateful people want to be participants in life, not spectators. They are more optimistic and attract healthy relationships. While we may not avoid health issues completely, a positive attitude does strengthen us physiologically and provides more opportunity for healing. This proved true through the healing I've experienced in my own life.

Something I find interesting and wonderful is that gratitude leads to the development of a spiritual life, and spirituality encourages gratitude. Some experiences can be seen only as blessings. I know there are those who may call it luck or coincidence when something good happens. Those feelings may create happiness in the moment, but they do not fill us with joy, hope and expectation for the future. Wherever you are on your spiritual journey, allow your blessings to strengthen and grow you spiritually. See yourself designing your life in tandem with your divine guidance. Express gratitude for your blessings, large and small, and allow yourself to experience the joy and hope that come from that simple act of faith.

We all have lost someone we loved and cherished. Our hearts ache over the void created by their absence. Our minds seem unable to focus on even the simplest aspects of life. We need to allow ourselves to grieve. I was with my mother when she passed. The heartache I felt in that moment seemed almost more than I could bear, and it continued for several days. Then, as I sat in the airport, waiting to board a flight home, I began scripting memories of wonderful, fun, special times I had shared with my mother. As I remembered and wrote, my heart and soul began to fill with gratitude for all the time we had together. I continued writing in this journal of memories for a year as I walked through my healing process. My pain was replaced with gratitude, and although even now, nearly eleven years later, tears fill my eyes, my heart is filled with gratitude for those precious memories. Grieving is a natural and necessary process. It is my belief that staying immersed in it is not. Gratitude helps heal.

Joy

It is no accident that a chapter on gratitude follows one on joy. Being grateful creates joy in our lives. Whenever someone tells me they have no joy in their lives, I ask what they are grateful for, and I often learn they have not even thought of or expressed gratitude in quite some time. We can get so entrenched in the problem side of life that we miss the blessings. Or, we may be so focused on that one big "ask" we have put out to God and the Universe that we miss the smaller blessings happening every day. I truly believe that most people would rather live joyful lives but make hard work of it. Or they give away their joy but believe it is being stolen from them.

The truth is, joy is available to each of us, but we must make choices that open the door for it to fill our lives. Expressing gratitude creates joy. A grateful heart and mind cannot help feeling joy. Walking in faith through all of life's situations also brings joy, because there is freedom in knowing that we have trusted God's Divine Intelligence with the desires of our hearts. Whether we are simply asking for a positive attitude today or for healing for ourselves or a loved one, we can experience the joy of knowing we are leaning into God's perfect answer coming to us under grace and in God's perfect timing. Being tied to or manipulating results can be exhausting; it allows us to engage in fear and doubt and closes the door to experiencing our joy.

I have heard people say that another person, such as a spouse, family member, friend or coworker, steals their joy, and that every time they are happy about something, this person finds a way to ruin it for them. This is a mistaken view of joy. First of all, they are confusing "happiness with joy. Happiness is fleeting. It is created in a moment, but the moment doesn't last forever. Joy is lasting; it is the knowledge and wisdom that Divine Intelligence is working in every situation of our lives for our highest and best good. I also don't believe another person can steal our joy. If joy leaves us, I believe it is because we gave it away. I have often pointed this out to clients who were blaming someone for robbing them of all their joy. We cannot control the attitudes and actions of those around us, but we are definitely in control of the effect they have on us and how we respond. We may be blindsided by the words or actions of another. We may allow ourselves to feel hurt, anger, fear or resentment in the moment, but we do not want to hook that feeling and allow it to manifest. When we flip that switch and go for a better thought and feeling, we begin invoking divine guidance and manifesting a better outcome. Believe it or not, that is a demonstration of a joyful life because you have not given the power of your thoughts, feelings and outcome to someone else. How that person processes life is their choice. We cannot choose joy for another, but we definitely have the power to claim our joy and allow it to manifest and demonstrate in our own lives.

Hope

So, we know gratitude produces joy. What, then, comes from joy? The product of joy is hope! Often clients tell me what they want: a loving relationship, a rewarding job. As they do there is a feeling of low energy in their voice. Sometimes they sound sad, even angry, as they describe what they want. Even in everyday conversations we hear friends, family and coworkers talk about what they want from life. People will say "I just want" or "for once, I want…" When the word want is used, feelings, thoughts and beliefs are coming from a place of lack or need. Want keeps goals or desires out in a seemingly unattainable future, leaving the person feeling deficient and sometimes defeated or uninspired. Want definitely does not come from a place of joy. Often those who spend their lives wanting and wishing are not expressing gratitude for the good already in their lives and haven't experienced the joy that results from a grateful heart. As a result, they may not feel deserving of a hopeful life, but of course they are.

Enough said about want. Let's talk about hope! Hope connects us to anticipation, aspiration and, yes, expectation! Hope does not leave us with feelings of lack or defeat but allows us to keep our goals clearly in site. When obstacles appear, hope does not allow us to wallow in the problem but rather to search for solutions, so that our expected outcome manifests and demonstrates in our physical world. Even when we are in distress and tempted to walk in fear, hope gives us the courage and motivation to step out in faith, finding a way to navigate a pathway to success. Living a hopeful life means we are following divine direction to our expected outcome. We will receive all we need, (courage, patience, confidence) to take the action required on our part to achieve our goals.

Hope is inspiring and empowering! Research has shown there is a physiological effect in the body when a person is hopeful. The brain releases phytochemicals called enkephalins and endorphins. These are the feel- good hormones, or happy hormones. Runners know them as the "runner's high." These chemicals also block pain and speed up the healing process. We should always speak and think messages of hope over our lives and into our desires. An example of this would be, perfect healing is coming to me now, under grace and in divine timing. When we do this, our anticipation builds, and we begin to see and believe that our goals and desires are becoming our truth. This is truly engaging the law of attraction! We begin to attract everyone and everything necessary to manifest our goals.

From my personal, spiritual point of view, the Bible connects hope to God's promises for my life being fulfilled. It is Divine Intelligence that creates the opportunities and opens the doors for us to walk through gratefully, joyfully and hopefully.

Attitude

Attitude, whether positive or negative, is a choice. The attitude we choose affects every other choice in life. We may be faced with an unpleasant or undesirable situation—even a seemingly impossible problem—but if we change our perception of the situation we can change our attitude about its outcome. When we stop spinning negative thoughts and wishing things or people were different, it is easier to choose positive thoughts and solutions. When we choose to see positive results, we are choosing a positive attitude.

Remember: Where thought goes, energy flows. When our thoughts are positive, what we believe and hope about an outcome will be positive as well. The important point is to recognize when you are unhappy or carrying a negative attitude. Change the way you respond or react to people and situations. When you do, the outcome will be different.

We are all born with a clean slate, but we are not the first person to write on it. Our parents, teachers, siblings and others write on our slates long before we do. Our perspective of life and who we are in it will be positive or negative depending on the details we have been taught and what we have learned from our life experiences. Some of us have seen and heard some very negative things. If you had this life experience, remember this: Your happiness, value and abundance in life are not dependent on the thoughts, words or actions of others. Your happiness is your choice, so speak release over any negativity others may have poured into you. Forgive all of it, forgive them, and forgive yourself for having let it rob your life of the happiness, joy and abundance that is yours to receive under grace and in divine timing.

Remember how powerful your words are in creating every aspect of your life. Find affirmations that are meaningful to you and speak them over events and encounters with others throughout your day, beginning the moment you wake up. This sets you up to recognize, receive and rejoice, making it easy to choose and maintain your positive attitude.

Take a look at the people who are in your life on a regular basis. How do they speak about themselves and others? Being with people who are always complaining—about themselves, life or others—is a drain on your positive energy. I realize there may be one or two you cannot avoid completely, but minimize the time you spend with them, and don't engage in their negative conversations. It is so important that we surround ourselves with other positive people who are living hopeful, joyful lives. Seek out people who, like you, are choosing a positive attitude toward life.

Purpose

I often hear people say they are searching for their purpose in life. The fact is, our purpose isn't a goal or a thing that is somewhere other than where we are. Our intended purpose is right here in the moment and situation where we find ourselves. Whether the situation is challenging, edifying or mundane, our purpose is to allow Divine Intelligence to guide our thoughts, words and actions as we live and walk through the situation. Our purpose, then, is to apply the knowledge and wisdom of the experience to grow and become the person we are meant to be.

Can you see how we and our purpose are always evolving? Our purpose is a process of growing, learning, teaching, receiving and giving back. We each have our own divinely ordained purpose. When we focus on walking in that Divine flow, fulfilling our purpose in the moment, we are co-creating, with God, the wonderful lives we are meant to live, as well as having a positive impact on the lives of others.

To believe we are here to fulfill only one objective in the course of our lives is to cheat ourselves of the rich learning and teaching experiences of each moment. We each have unique gifts, and they will manifest and demonstrate magnificently if we live fully in the present. What we think, say and do right now is creating the life we will live in the future. What do you want your future to be? Remember: Where thought goes, energy flows. Whatever we are radiating out into the world we are attracting back into our lives. Living with purpose right now creates an abundance of purpose tomorrow, next month and next year. That is an exciting thought, and I have created an abundant, purposeful life by living fully in the present moment.

People often confuse purpose with a profession, a talent or a calling. The truth is, living purposefully each moment will lead us on a life path of discovery that discloses a profession as well as talents we may develop. By living on purpose, I have pursued and enjoyed three very different career paths, each lasting several years and often overlapping. If you are vigilant and living on purpose each moment, amazing opportunities present themselves. It is so important that we remain open to learning, teaching and growing. When we are in a situation that is challenging, part of our purpose is to learn and grow through it. Don't stay stuck by asking "why me" or by wallowing in sadness or anger. Make a note of what you are learning. Someday you may be the teacher for someone else in a similar situation. When life is exciting, enjoy it, share it and accept every blessing you are receiving.

The bottom line is this: We are not meant to coast through life waiting for our purpose to show up or for someone else to define it for us. We don't need to label situations as good or bad, right or wrong. If we are living purposefully in each moment, knowing divine guidance is always available to us, we will learn and teach those things we are meant to learn and teach, and we will live the abundant lives we are intended to live.

Success and Abundance

For me, the principles I have outlined in the preceding sections, when practiced faithfully, continue to add up to a life of success and abundance. I know I am always just one choice away from receiving my next blessing. I believe God has already made manifest every good and perfect destination for me. I need to choose to open my mind, heart and spirit to receive them in God's right timing. I name the desires of my heart and simply say, "I am open to receive, and I am receiving this or something better." Don't allow flawed, negative thinking to get in the way of receiving your abundance. Release those thoughts and replace them with thoughts and visions of abundance flowing into your life. Don't forget to thank God for the abundance you already have. Gratitude keeps our hearts open. When we are grateful, we cannot help being aware of the abundance in our lives.

Taking time, often, to sit quietly and observe each area of our lives is an excellent way to see and appreciate our past and present success and abundance. Look at relationships and situations where you were blessed with love and patience that helped resolve issues. Take time to appreciate the blessing of courage to love, bless and release a relationship, job or opportunity that was not for your highest and best good. Instead of complaining about your job, your home or your financial status, find something for which you are grateful. Greater abundance and success cannot come to us when we are in a state of ingratitude. This is a truth I have proved. The truth I now choose to prove is that gratitude as a way of living opens the doors to my own divinely manifested success and abundance.

Some people say that to desire success, abundance and prosperity is selfish or greedy. Let me clarify this as simply as I possibly can. I do not affirm my success and abundance with a selfish or greedy heart or mindset. I do affirm, however, that I enjoy success and have abundance to share and spare! I also give thanks that I am blessed and am a blessing to others. Hoarding our abundance in any area of life will stop our flow. It is only when we share our love, joy, talents and finances that they are promised to be returned, pressed down and multiplied. We should not give with the sole intent of getting. That would be coming from a place of greed. Rather, when we allow our blessings to bless others as well, the divine source will flow even more blessings into our lives. We don't make it happen. It simply works that way.

Take a moment to sit quietly on a regular basis. See clearly with your mind's eye what your successful, abundant life looks like. Let it fill your heart with gratitude for the abundance you currently enjoy as well as the even greater abundance you are about to receive. If you live your life with this gratitude, your relationships will be healthier and stronger. Challenges will come with solutions. Doors of opportunity will open to pathways of success and prosperity. You may discover you are making choices with ease and courage that now reward you with abundant, good health. Don't covet another's success and abundance. Be happy others are blessed and know that the divine is manifesting your blessings. It is up to you to believe it, and to open your heart, mind and spirit to receive success and abundance in every area of your life.

Scripting Your Life

When we are creating our lives, our thoughts are powerful, the spoken word is more powerful, and our written word is most powerful. There is something about writing and reading our goals and desires that gives them life. I have scripted in a journal for several years. If you haven't, I hope you will begin. Scripting is the single best action you can take to gain clarity, establish commitment and create the life you desire having and love living.

When you write, state your desires as though they already have come to pass. This brings them into the present. Saying things like "I want" or "someday" keeps the desire out of reach. Be detailed and specific as you write. This will help you recognize your best life choices as you are turning your desire into a reality. If something doesn't come into being immediately, don't spend time in worry. Know that your desire or something better is coming to you. Also, know that even though you have written down a specific desire, you are always free to amend it. You are not only the author; you are also the editor of your life. Remember, Divine Intelligence is always growing us and expanding our horizons. We want to be open to receive whatever abundance, joy, success and prosperity are being made manifest in our lives. What we affirm today may not show up for some time, but there may be opportunities opening up that are preparing you for the fulfillment of your affirmation or something even better!

As you are writing, dare to expand your thinking. Let yourself see the bigger picture of your life, the greater achievement and abundance. When we do this, we are then able to write in detail the action we will take and what the journey will look like. I did this when I was in the mortgage banking industry and envisioning my success was still very new to me. I knew I hoped to be the top producer, so I pictured myself studying information specific to the industry and talking to those who were already successful in the industry. I believed I learned and easily applied the knowledge in order to become the top producer, and that's exactly what I did. Many years later, when I wanted to change careers and become a massage therapist, I spent five years seeing and writing out in detail how I would make that transition, how I would pay for school and how I would learn all that was necessary to be the very best, most successful therapist. When I was in school, I began scripting the details of my practice, the physical location, the floor plan of my wellness center, the quality and number of other therapists I would bring into my center and the clients I would attract. All of it and more came to be. My scripting opened new doors of opportunity, and I began to write about those and to watch with gratitude and excitement as my life continued evolving in magnificent directions.

Remember, you are the author and editor of your life so don't neglect scripting about your personal life. I was single for several years and had scripted that I was happily unmarried, and I was. There came a point I decided to edit that vision. I could see the possibility of desiring a loving relationship with a man one day, so I began editing my personal vision for my life. I scripted that God helped me to want a relationship and then that a loving, trustworthy man was coming into my life. As I shared earlier here, this all came to fruition, and we have been happily married for fifteen years. Our desires change as we grow through life, and God is always listening, so be specific and use your editing power when you change your vision. Always affirm, clearly, that you are open to receiving— and *are* receiving—all the good God is sending to you now!

If even one of the principles I have outlined resonates with you, I hope it helps you to "Love Your Life and Expect the Best".

Love and blessings on your journey.

Marlene Fuller Svoboda
Personal and Professional Life Coach
Ordained Interfaith Minister
marlenefsvoboda@gmail.com

Affirmations

Following are just a few of my own affirmations. I use these and many others in my meditations and prayers as well as throughout the day. I have found courage, peace, forgiveness, love, gratitude, joy and hope by affirming the power of God to make manifest all I need and desire that is good and perfect in my life.

Feel free to use these affirmations in your life or allow them to inspire your own perfect and personal affirmations. You will be amazed how they will change your thoughts and words about a situation in an instant. You may repeat an affirmation many times if you find your thoughts returning to a situation. That's fine. You will be reinforcing your openness to receive your perfect blessings.

As I give this day to God, I know I open my heart, mind and spirit to blessings beyond measure.

There are no limits on God's spiritual energy.

I listen to Spirit with ease and openness.

I find myself seeking Spirit's guidance before all else.

I know Divine Guidance has the perfect plan in place for me.

Opening the door to my soul allows me to radiate love, grace and joy, putting the law of attraction in action and returning love, grace and joy to me in great abundance.

I am authentically who I am meant to be.

I make healthy choices.

My life is rich, full and blessed, and I am grateful.

Nothing and no one can keep me from my perfect good or keep my perfect good from coming to me now. It is so, and so it is. Thank You, God.

As I trust Spirit, I am free to release, let go and know my intention is working with God's perfect design to create my highest and best good.

I am one with God, and God is one with me.

As I trust God's Divine Intelligence, I grow in courage.

I release and let go of the past knowing my future is rich, full and good.

Gratitude brings hope into my world, and hope brings joy.

Courage and compassion are my companions as I walk through life with God.

I radiate and receive positive energy.

I celebrate who I am and what I have accomplished, am accomplishing and have yet to accomplish.

I am guided by Divine Wisdom.

My eyes and heart are open to see the beauty all around me.

My vision of my purpose becomes clear as I come to understand that everything I do has purpose.

I am a visible, vibrant woman (man/person).

Divine Intelligence clears my path of all debris as I walk easily toward my goals.

I place the journey of my soul at the forefront of my life's path.

My mind, heart and spirit are filled with gratitude.

I am grateful for the peace I feel in this moment.

God provides a clear path and gives me the vision, ability and desire to live my purpose now.

I live my life with grace, confidence and style.

I extend and receive love, blessings and grace in my relationships.

I love my life, and I expect the best.

References

Sermon on the Mount by Emmet Fox
Harper Collins Publishers 1989

Bible
New Living Translation

As a Man Thinketh by James Allen
Publisher: Barnes and Noble Books 1992

The Seven Spiritual Laws of Success by Deepak
Chopra
Publisher: New World Library 1994

The Dynamic Laws of Prosperity by Catherine
Ponder
DeVors & Company Publishing 1995

Stake Your Claim by Emmet Fox
Harper & Row Publishers 1952

The Game of Life and How To Play It
By Florence Scovill Shin
De Vors & Company Publishing
Copyright 1925

Notes

Notes

Notes